ANIMAL FAMILIES / FAMILIAS DE ANIMALES

GORILLAS / GORILAS
LIFE IN THE TROOP / VIDA EN LA MANADA

Willow Clark   Traducción al español: Eduardo Alamán

PowerKiDS
press.
New York

Published in 2011 by The Rosen Publishing Group, Inc.
29 East 21st Street, New York, NY 10010

First Edition

Editor: Jennifer Way   Traducción al español: Eduardo Alamán
Book Design: Julio Gil

Photo Credits: Cover, pp. 10–11, 17, 19, 21, 24 (top right) Shutterstock.com; back cover © www. iStockphoto.com/Kristijan Hranisavljevic; pp. 5, 24 (bottom right) Hemera/Thinkstock; p. 7 Photos.com/ Thinkstock; pp. 9, 12–13, 24 (bottom left) iStockphoto/Thinkstock; pp. 15, 24 (top left) Andy Rouse/Getty Images; p. 23 Andrew Plumptre/Getty Images.

Library of Congress Cataloging-in-Publication Data

Clark, Willow.
  [Gorillas. Spanish & English]
  Gorillas = Gorilas : life in the troop : vida en la manada / by Willow Clark. — 1st ed.
      p. cm. — (Animal families = Familias de animales)
  Includes index.
  ISBN 978-1-4488-3127-2 (library binding)
  1. Gorilla—Juvenile literature. 2. Familial behavior in animals—Juvenile literature. I. Title. II. Title: Gorilas.
  QL737.P96C5818 2011
  599.884–dc22
                                        2010026112

Manufactured in the United States of America

CPSIA Compliance Information: Batch #WW11PK: For Further Information contact Rosen Publishing, New York, New York at 1-800-237-9932

Web Sites: Due to the changing nature of Internet links, PowerKids Press has developed an online list of Web sites related to the subject of this book. This site is updated regularly. Please use this link to access the list: www.powerkidslinks.com/afam/gorilla/

CONTENTS

CONTENIDO

Gorillas live in Africa. A family of gorillas is called a **troop**.

Los gorilas viven en África. Las familias de gorilas viven en grupos llamados **manadas**.

Troops have one or two young males. Troops also have females and their young.

Las manadas tienen uno o dos gorilas machos. Las manadas también tienen hembras y jóvenes gorilas.

An older male gorilla is the troop leader. He is called the **silverback**.

El líder de la manada es un gorila macho adulto. A estos se les llama gorilas de **espalda plateada**.

The silverback is the biggest
and strongest of all the
gorillas in the troop.

Los gorilas de espalda
plateada son los más fuertes y
más grandes de las manadas.

Gorillas spend most of their day looking for food. They eat plants, bugs, and worms.

Los gorilas pasan la mayoría del tiempo buscando comida. Los gorilas comen plantas, insectos y gusanos.

When the troop is resting, the members **groom** each other.

Cuando las manadas descansan, sus miembros se **limpian** unos a otros.

Each member of the troop makes a sleeping **nest**. Mother gorillas hold their babies.

Cada miembro de la manada hace un **nido** para dormir. Las mamás gorila abrazan a sus bebés.

Baby gorillas ride on their mothers' backs for the first two or three years of their lives.

Los bebé gorila montan en la espalda de sus mamás durante los tres primeros años de vida.

Young gorillas play while their mothers watch them.

Las mamás gorila vigilan a sus bebés mientras juegan.

Gorillas leave the troop when they are 8 to 11 years old. They join a new troop.

Los gorilas dejan la manada entre los 8 y los 11 años de edad. Entonces se unen a una nueva manada.

Words to Know / Palabras que debes saber

groom / limpiar

nest / (el) nido

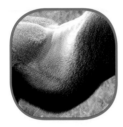

silverback
(la) espalda plateada

troop / (la) manada

24